BORROWING BUNNIES

A SURPRISING TRUE TALE OF FOSTERING RABBITS

NEWBERY HONOR AUTHOR
CYNTHIA LORD

PHOTOGRAPHS BY
JOHN BALD

ILLUSTRATIONS BY
HAZEL MITCHELL

FARRAR STRAUS GIROUX

NEW YORK

To Cottontail Cottage Rabbit Rescue,
for all you do for bunnies —C.L.

For my father, who bought me my first camera —J.B.

To my first bunny, Scrub Bud —H.M.

Farrar Straus Giroux Books for Young Readers
An imprint of Macmillan Publishing Group, LLC
175 Fifth Avenue, New York, NY 10010

Text copyright © 2019 by Cynthia Lord
Photographs copyright © 2019 by John Bald
Illustrations copyright © 2019 by Hazel Mitchell

Color separations by Bright Arts (H.K.) Ltd.
Printed in China by Toppan Leefung Printing Ltd.,
Dongguan City, Guangdong Province
Designed by Monique Sterling
First edition, 2019
10 9 8 7 6 5 4 3 2 1

mackids.com

Library of Congress Control Number: 2018020381
ISBN: 978-0-374-30841-4

Our books may be purchased in bulk for promotional, educational, or
business use. Please contact your local bookseller or the Macmillan Corporate
and Premium Sales Department at (800) 221-7945 ext. 5442 or by email at
MacmillanSpecialMarkets@macmillan.com.

My family fosters bunnies for an animal rescue. That means that we take care of the bunnies at our home for a few months until they're ready to be adopted by another family. Some bunnies we foster have never lived in a home or been loved. It's our job to teach them how to be good pets for their new family.

You could say that we borrow bunnies!

Bunnies are all different, and fostering is full of surprises. After a few days of feeling safe and loved, a bunny that had seemed shy at first might be cuddling with me and leaping off the furniture! Being surprised by the bunnies is a fun part of fostering.

One pair of Netherland Dwarf bunnies gave us the biggest surprise of all. These two bunnies had lived hard lives outdoors in wire cages covered only by a tarp, even in snowy weather. When they arrived at the rescue, they were hungry, thirsty, and scared. First, they were given food, water, and good care. Then, the bunnies needed to learn how to live in a home. They needed to see that people could be kind.

The rescue called me.

I brought home a little gray bunny named **Benjamin** and a chocolate-brown bunny named **Peggotty**.

I gave each one a pen with food, water, hay, toys, a litter box, and a rabbit-sized wooden house.

Peggotty had a drink of water and a rest, but Benjamin was eager to explore and meet my own two bunnies, Blueberry and Muffin. He wanted all the bunnies to pay attention to him, and if they didn't, he **stamped his foot!**

Benjamin

Blueberry

Muffin

BAM

Since Benjamin was a boy and Peggotty was a girl, they couldn't live in the same pen. But they liked to visit each other and touch noses.

Every day, I stroked Benjamin and Peggotty to show them that people can be kind. I taught them to use litter boxes to keep their pens clean. They discovered new treats—like bananas.

When a bunny is happy, it leaps into the air and twists. That's called a binky. The first time I saw Benjamin and Peggotty binky, I grinned. They were doing so well! They had learned to live in a home and to trust people. I could see they were happy. I thought they would soon be ready to be adopted.

That's when I got a **BIG** surprise.

One morning I noticed that Peggotty had filled her little house with fur and fleece from the bottom of her pen.

When I lifted the house to look inside, **the fur wiggled**.

WE HAD FOUR BABY BUNNIES!

They looked like miniature hippos!

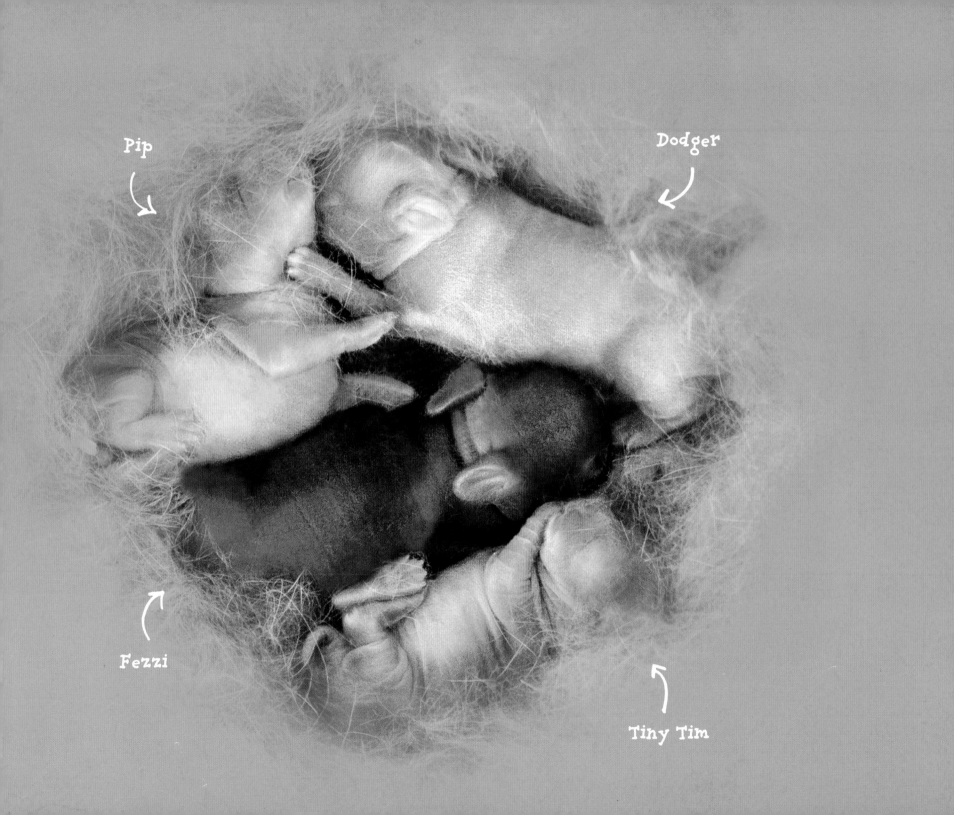

Pip

Dodger

Fezzi

Tiny Tim

The name "Peggotty" comes from a book by Charles Dickens. So we named the babies for Dickens characters, too. **Fezzi** (short for Fezziwig) was the dark-brown baby. The light-colored one was **Dodger**. **Pip** was reddish brown, and the littlest baby was **Tiny Tim**.

Oliver Twist

Great Expectations

A Christmas Carol

DAVID COPPERFIELD

I checked on them as Peggotty hopped around the room. I gave her some carrot tops and told her she was a **good mama**.

Every day, Dodger and Fezzi changed. As their fur grew, they stopped looking like baby hippos. Instead, they looked like **tiny bunnies**.

But Pip and Tiny Tim were not born well and strong. We helped them nurse before Dodger and Fezzi to be sure they got enough to eat. We tucked them between their stronger siblings to keep them warm.

We asked the rescue and our veterinarian for help and tried everything they suggested. But Tiny Tim lived only a few days, and Pip died soon after.

My heart was broken.

For a while after Pip and Tiny Tim died, I felt both happy and sad whenever Dodger or Fezzi did something new. I was happy that Dodger and Fezzi were healthy, curious baby bunnies, but I was sad that Pip and Tiny Tim hadn't had the chance to grow up, too.

Fezzi and Dodger learned to
eat hay, drink water, **sniff**,

climb,

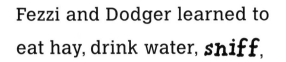

and **hop**.

They played with toys and a tunnel.

They even liked to cuddle with
two stuffed-animal bunnies.
We named those toy bunnies
Pip and Tiny Tim.

Whirrr! Whirrr!

Ding-Dong!

Dodger and Fezzi heard interesting sounds at our house: the doorbell, the television, music, and—*the vacuum cleaner!*

They explored new places. They visited Benjamin and **touched noses**.

Tweet! Tweet!

The first time I took Fezzi and Dodger outdoors, a breeze was blowing.
They felt earth and grass under their paws. They heard cars going by,
our neighbor hammering, a dog barking, and birds singing.

During each new experience, Fezzi and Dodger were shy at first.

Then brave.

Fezzi and Dodger kept growing and
growing and GROWING!

I touched and held each of the bunnies every day. I also invited others to hold them so they wouldn't be afraid of new people.

After being fostered in our home for eight weeks, Fezzi, Dodger, Peggotty, and Benjamin were ready to be adopted. They had all learned how to live in a home and be good pets.

For a long time, Peggotty would hop over and rub her chin on my foot whenever she was out of her pen. That's a bunny's way of saying "You belong to me." Then, if I reached for her, she would dart away. But now, after she rubbed her chin on me, she'd put her head down for me to pet, asking me to love her back.

I had some mixed-up feelings, as you always do when getting ready to say goodbye. These bunnies had changed my life as much as I'd changed theirs.

Fezzi was the first one to be adopted. She went home with a wonderful family. I sent her off with a bag full of familiar toys and things that smelled like her bunny family, including one of the stuffed-animal bunnies.

Then Dodger and Peggotty were adopted together by a family with two daughters.

That left Benjamin. As I thought about finding a home for him, I got another surprise. I realized that Benjamin already had a home . . .

WITH US!

Welcome HOME!

My family adopted Benjamin, and now he's ours—**for keeps**.

DO YOU WANT YOUR OWN RABBIT FOR KEEPS?

A rabbit can be a wonderful pet. But bringing any pet into your home is a big decision. You should research information about rabbits, and then ask yourself these questions. Maybe you'll want to adopt your own bunny—for keeps!

Is anyone in your family allergic to rabbits or timothy hay? All pet rabbits must eat timothy hay. It helps wear down their teeth and keep their tummies healthy.

Do you have young siblings? If there is a baby or toddler in your family, it's best to wait a few years before getting a pet rabbit. Rabbits require a lot of care, and they are easily hurt and frightened. So they are a better pet for older children and adults.

Do you have time for a rabbit? Every day, your rabbit will need a clean pen, food, water, hay, and exercise. A rabbit also needs companionship, whether from you or another rabbit.

Are you ready to take care of your rabbit for many years? A healthy rabbit can live eight to twelve years!

Do you have the money for a rabbit? In addition to paying an adoption fee, you'll need to buy a pen, a litter box, toys, and dishes for food and water, and to make regular purchases of bedding, hay, and food. You will also need to take your rabbit to a veterinarian if he or she gets sick or hurt.

Can you keep your rabbit safe? Some rabbits like to be petted, but some don't. They can get hurt if you drop them. They can be frightened by loud noises, rough handling, or being chased by other pets in your home. An unhappy or scared rabbit can't growl like a dog to say, "I don't like this." A rabbit can only stomp, run away, or bite. So creating a safe, quiet space for your rabbit and following good rules about playing with and handling him or her will keep everyone safe and happy—

and hoppy!